D1138286

"¡HABLO ESPAÑOL!"

CREATIVE ACTIVITIES
TO TEACH
BASIC SPANISH

BY LYNN BRISSON

Incentive Publications, Inc.
Nashville, Tennessee

Illustrated by Lynn Brisson
Cover by Marta Drayton
Edited by Leslie Britt and Karla Westerman

ISBN 0-86530-311-8

PRINTED IN THE UNITED STATES OF AMERICA

Table of Contents

INTRODUCTION

An increasing number of elementary schools are adding foreign language programs to their curricula, knowing that young children have a natural ability to learn and appreciate new languages. "¡Hablo Español!" was written as a companion resource for the elementary school language program. Students complete worksheets designed to teach and reinforce beginning Spanish vocabulary, which are then inserted into individual activity books.

The lessons introduce Spanish vocabulary: numbers, colors, days and months, school supplies, parts of the body, and fruits. The activities themselves are interactive; students must cut, color, and paste to construct each worksheet. As well, the final product on each page is often movable, allowing students to manipulate the pieces while reviewing new terms and self-checking their answers. (Younger children may need help with some of the cutting, pasting, and constructing.) Each activity contains a list of materials, and all of the necessary patterns are ready to reproduce and hand out to students.

A set of pronunciation cards has been designed to accompany each activity. The cards list the English word, the Spanish word, and the Spanish pronunciation for each vocabulary word studied. Students keep their pronunciation cards in a specially-designed pocket inserted into the activity booklet.

Research activities, which can be adapted to meet the needs and ability levels of your students, have also been included. Each research-based activity comes with a ready-to-reproduce worksheet. The final section of the book contains a motivating certificate of achievement and instructions for decorating an accompanying bulletin board.

"¡Hablo Español!" will introduce you to a fun-filled and rewarding method for introducing basic Spanish in your classroom. Before you know it, your students will stand up and proudly announce, "¡Hablo Español!"

BOOKLET COVER

MATERIALS:

- ◆ construction paper
- ◆ crayons or markers
- ◆ brads
- ◆ hole punch
- ◆ scissors

CONSTRUCTION:

1. Reproduce the booklet patterns on pages 8 and 9. Hand them out.

2. Have the students cut out the booklet covers and decorate them with crayons or markers.

3. Punch three holes along the side of each pattern and join with brads.

4. As students complete each activity, have them insert the pages in their booklets.

SPANISH
Activity Book

Name _____
(el nombre)

9

PRONUNCIATION CARDS

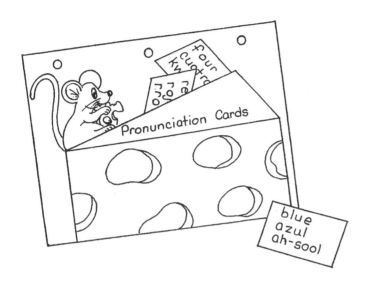

Pronunciation cards are provided for the words and phrases introduced in the activities. The pronunciation cards will help the students correctly pronounce the Spanish words. Before beginning each activity, review the pronunciation cards. Some of the Spanish words in the activities have *el, la, los, or las* before them. These words mean "the." Let students know that these articles are used in front of Spanish nouns, just as we use the word "the." The set of pronunciation cards follows the activity. Each pronunciation card contains the English word, the Spanish word, and the Spanish pronunciation.
Example:

blue	**English**
azul	**Spanish**
ah-sool	**Spanish Pronunciation**

MATERIALS:

◆ construction paper ◆ crayons ◆ paste ◆ hole punch ◆ scissors

CONSTRUCTION:

1. Reproduce the patterns on pages 11 and 12 and hand them out.

2. Have students cut out and color the patterns.

3. Students then paste the cheese pattern (page 12) to the activity page (page 11). This will create a pocket for the cards.

4. The completed worksheet can be inserted into the student booklet to serve as a pocket for storing each activity's pronunciation cards.

GLUE

11

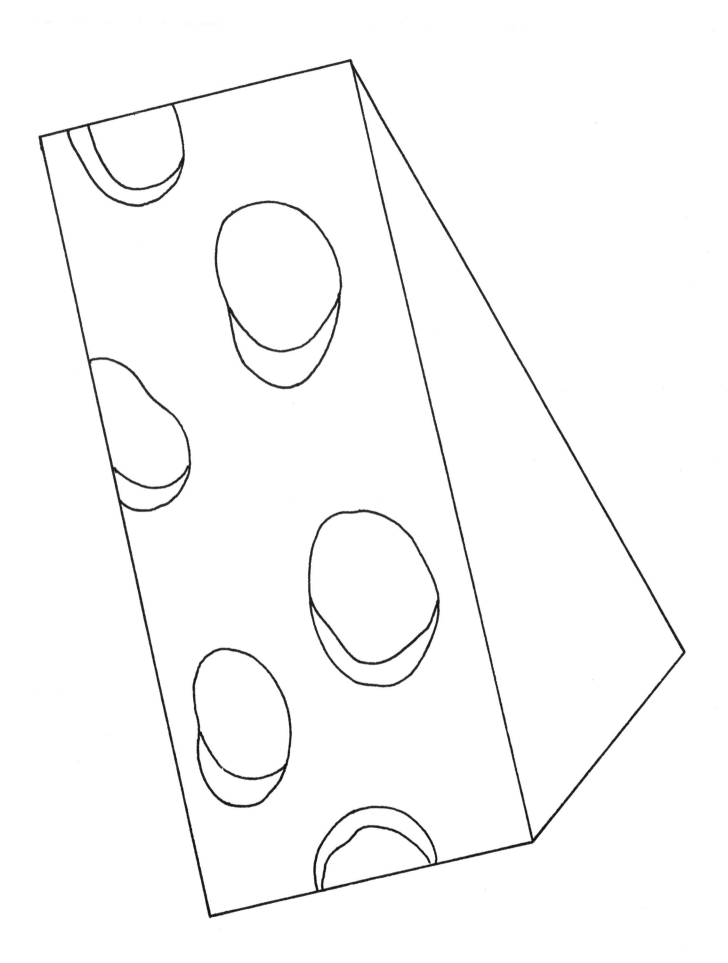

12 ©1995 by Incentive Publications, Inc., Nashville, TN.

COUNTING

MATERIALS:

- ◆ construction paper
- ◆ crayons
- ◆ paste
- ◆ hole punch
- ◆ scissors

CONSTRUCTION:

1. Reproduce the patterns on pages 14 and 15 and hand them out.

2. Have students cut out the patterns. Instruct them to color the mouse pattern (page 15) and then paste it to the activity page (page 14) to form a pocket.

3. Students cut apart the number cards from the pattern on page 15 and place the cards in the pocket.

4. Punch three holes along the side of the activity page.

5. The activity page is then inserted in the booklet.

6. Instruct the students to place the correct Spanish card from page 15 on the appropriate number on the activity page.

7. Pronunciation cards for this activity are on pages 16 and 17.

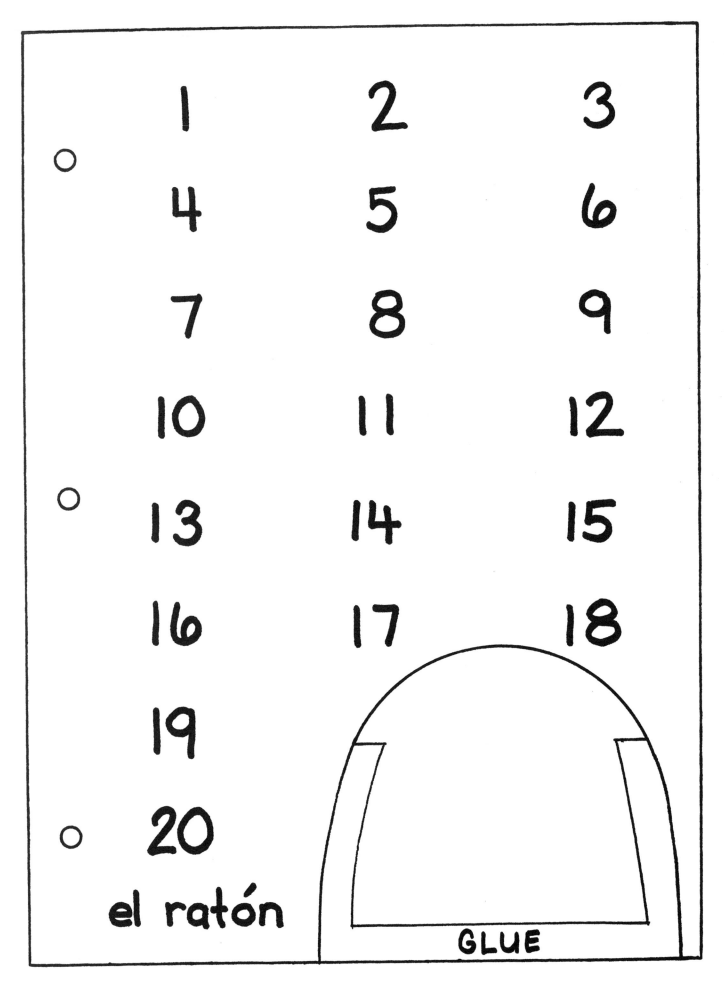

1 2 3

4 5 6

7 8 9

10 11 12

13 14 15

16 17 18

19

20

el ratón

GLUE

uno	dos	tres
cuatro	cinco	seis
siete	ocho	nueve
diez	once	doce
trece	catorce	quince
dieciséis	diecisiete	dieciocho
diecinueve		
veinte		

15

one **uno** oo–no	**two** **dos** dos	**three** **tres** trays
four **cuatro** kwah–tro	**five** **cinco** seen–ko	**six** **seis** says
seven **siete** seeay–tay	**eight** **ocho** o–cho	**nine** **nueve** nway–bay
ten **diez** dee–yes	**eleven** **once** on–say	**twelve** **doce** do–say

English	Spanish	Pronunciation
thirteen	trece	tray-say
fourteen	catorce	kah-tor-say
fifteen	quince	keen-say
sixteen	dieciséis	deeay-see-says
seventeen	diecisiete	deeay-see-seeay-tay
eighteen	dieciocho	deeay-see-o-cho
nineteen	diecinueve	deeay-see-nway-bay
twenty	veinte	bayn-tay
mouse	el ratón	el rrah-ton

COLORS

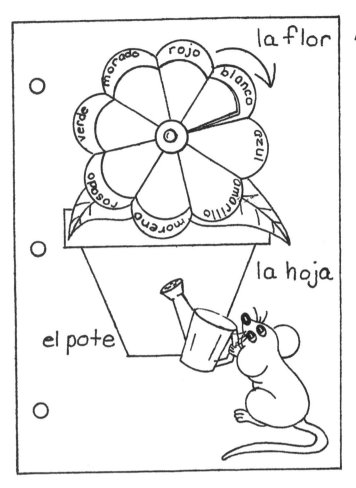

la flor

morado · rojo · blanco · azul · amarillo · moreno · rosado · verde

la hoja

el pote

MATERIALS:

◆ construction paper
◆ crayons
◆ brads
◆ hole punch
◆ scissors

CONSTRUCTION:

1. Reproduce the patterns on pages 19 and 20 and hand them out.

2. Students cut out the patterns, color the activity page (page 19), and color each petal (on page 20) according to the directions.

3. Punch a hole in each petal. Using a single brad, insert the brad through each petal, and then insert the brad through the center of the flower pattern (page 20).

4. Use the brad to attach the flower pattern and petals to the activity page.

5. Punch three holes along the side of the activity page.

6. Students insert the activity page in their booklets.

7. Each petal is turned to the corresponding word for review.

8. Pronunciation cards for this activity are on page 21.

la flor

la hoja

el tiesto

19

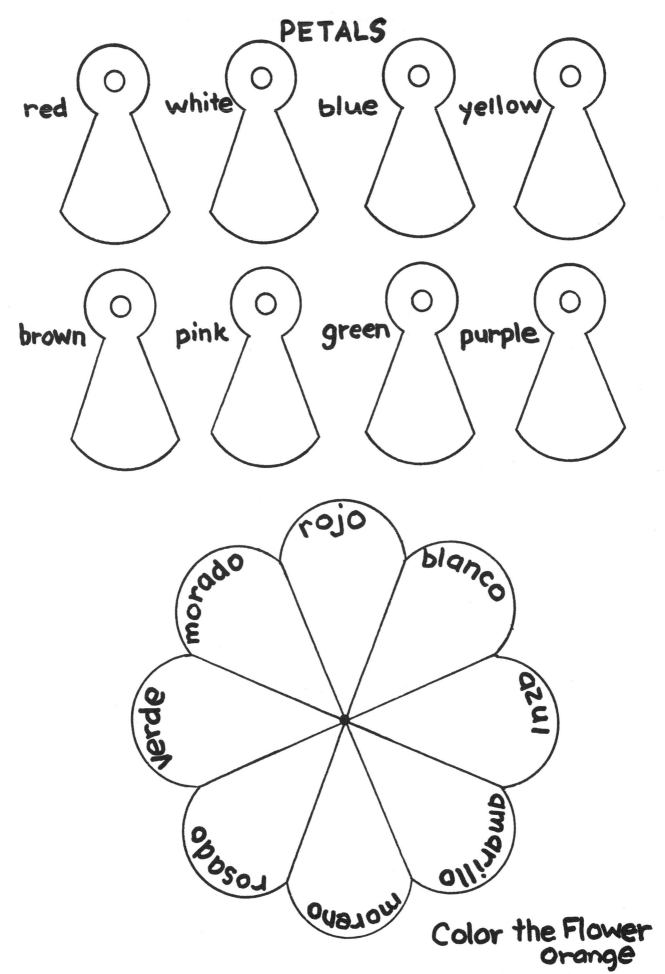

PETALS

red   white   blue   yellow

brown   pink   green   purple

Color the Flower
Orange

rojo
blanco
azul
amarillo
moreno
rosado
verde
morado

yellow
amarillo
ah–mah–ree–yo

green
verde
ber–day

flower
la flor
lah flohr

blue
azul
ah–sool

purple
morado
mo–rah–do

brown
moreno
mo–reh–no

leaf
la hoja
lah o–hah

red
rojo
rro–ho

white
blanco
blahn–ko

pink
rosado
rro–sah–do

pot
el pote
el po–tay

DAYS OF THE WEEK

MATERIALS:

- ◆ construction paper
- ◆ crayons
- ◆ paste
- ◆ hole punch
- ◆ brads
- ◆ scissors

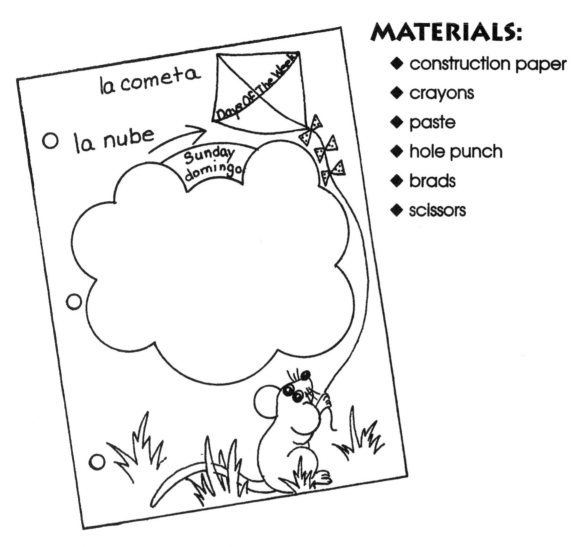

CONSTRUCTION:

1. Reproduce the patterns on pages 23 and 24 and hand them out.

2. Students color and cut out the patterns.

3. Insert a brad through the center of the circle pattern (page 24) and then attach to the cloud on the activity page (page 23).

4. Paste the cut-out cloud to the cloud on the activity page.
   Instruct students to place paste only around the outer edges of the cloud.

5. Punch three holes along the side of the activity page.

6. Students insert the activity page in their booklets.

7. The wheel is turned to review the days of the week.

8. Pronunciation cards for this activity are on page 25.

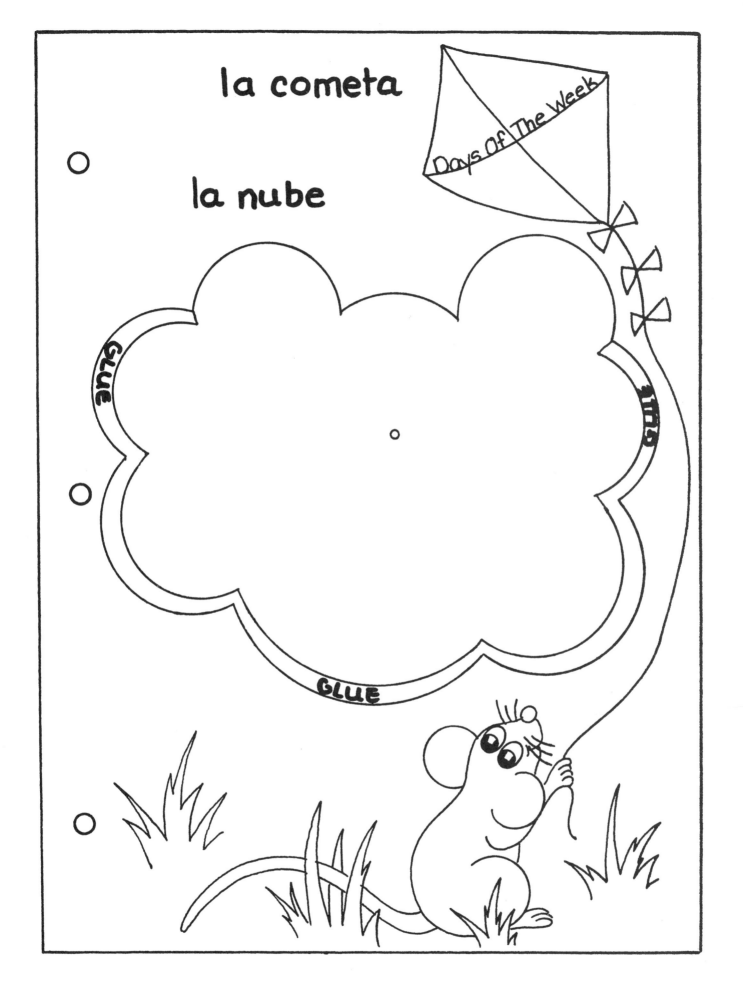

la cometa

la nube

Days Of The Week

GLUE

GLUE

GLUE

24

English	Spanish	Pronunciation
Sunday	domingo	doh-meen-goh
Monday	lunes	loo-nes
Tuesday	martes	mar-tes
Wednesday	miércoles	mee-air-koh-les
Thursday	jueves	whey-bes
Friday	viernes	bee-air-nes
Saturday	sábado	sah-bah-doh
cloud	la nube	lah noo-beh
kite	la cometa	lah ko-may-tah

MONTHS OF THE YEAR

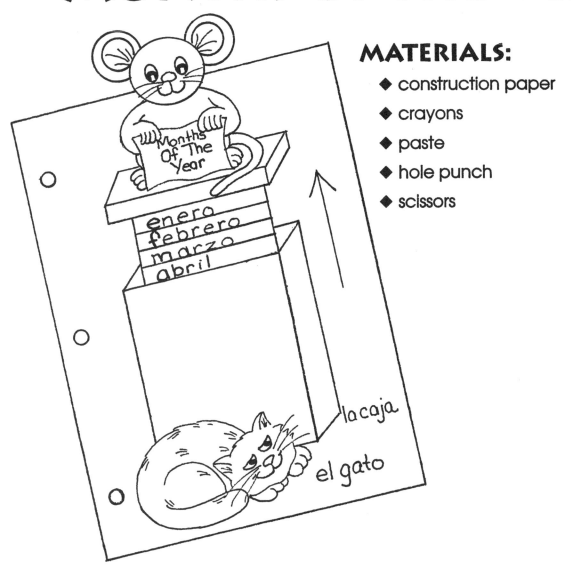

MATERIALS:

- ◆ construction paper
- ◆ crayons
- ◆ paste
- ◆ hole punch
- ◆ scissors

CONSTRUCTION:

1. Reproduce the patterns on pages 27 and 28 and hand them out for students to color and cut out.

2. Students cut a slit in the top of the the box pattern (page 27) along the dotted lines.

3. Instruct students to insert the tab pattern (page 28) in the box, paste the mouse pattern (page 28) to the top of the tab, and close the box.

4. Punch three holes along the side of the activity page (page 27).

5. Students insert the activity page in their booklets.

6. Instruct the students to say the months in Spanish and then pull up the mouse to self-check their answers.

7. Pronunciation cards for this activity are on pages 28 and 29.

la caja

el gato

27

GLUE
enero
febrero
marzo
abril
mayo
junio
julio
agosto
septiembre
octubre
noviembre
diciembre

Pronunciation Cards

cat el gato el gah-toh
box la caja lah cah-hah

Months Of The Year

January **enero** ay-nay-roh	**February** **febrero** fay-bray-roh	**March** **marzo** mar-soh
April **abril** ah-breel	**May** **mayo** mah-yoh	**June** **junio** hoo-nee-oh
July **julio** hoo-lee-oh	**August** **agosto** ah-gos-toh	**September** **septiembre** seh-tee-em-breh
October **octubre** ok-too-breh	**November** **noviembre** noh-bee-em-breh	**December** **diciembre** dee-see-em-breh

SCHOOL SUPPLIES

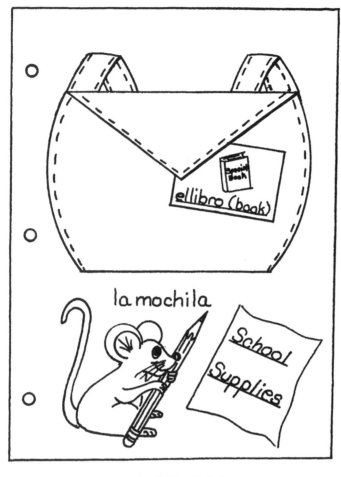

MATERIALS:

◆ paper
◆ crayons or colored pencils
◆ paste
◆ hole punch
◆ scissors

CONSTRUCTION:

1. Reproduce the activity patterns on pages 31–33 and hand them out.
2. Students color and cut out the activity page (page 31).
3. Students cut out the backpack pattern (page 32). Instruct them to turn the backpack over and color it.
4. Have students fold up the backpack along the straight line and paste both ends together. They will fold down the flap to close the backpack.
5. Students paste the backpack to the activity page.
6. Punch three holes along the side of the activity page.
7. Have students insert the activity page in their booklets.
8. Instruct the students to draw the appropriate pictures on their word cards (page 33) and cut them out.
9. Students should keep their word cards in the backpacks.
10. Pronunciation cards for this activity are on page 34.

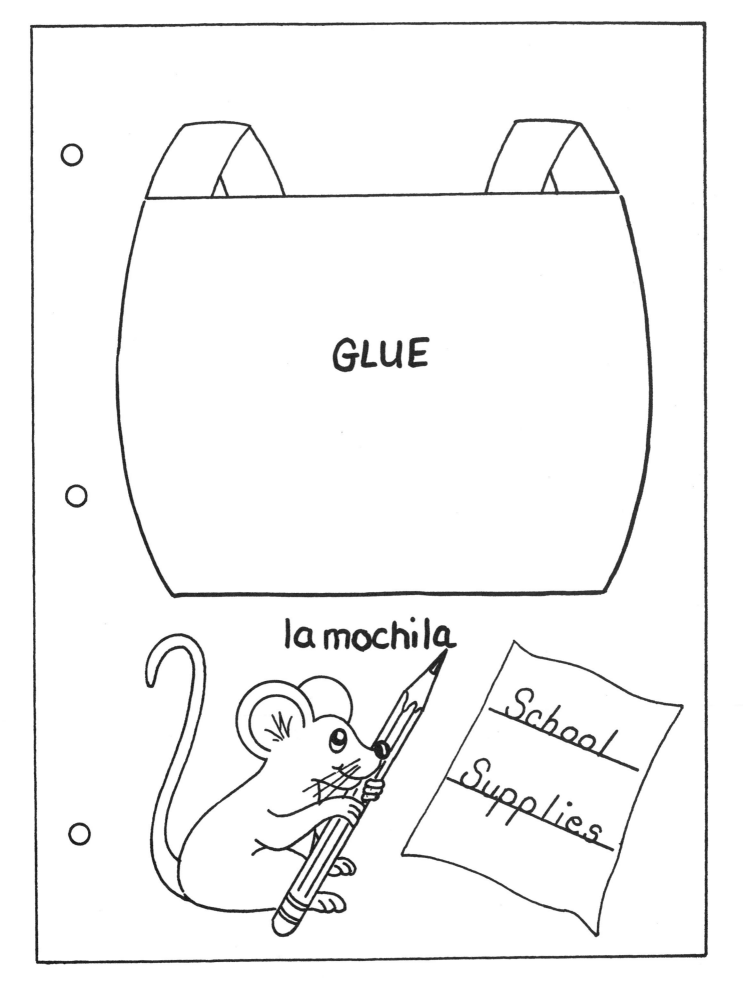

GLUE

la mochila

School Supplies

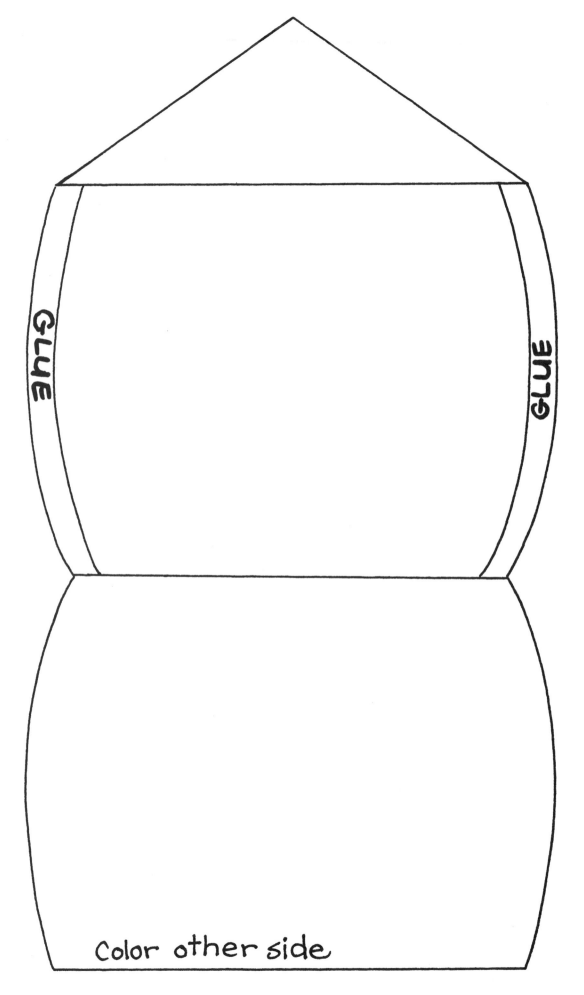

GLUE

GLUE

Color other side

el libro (book)	**la regla (ruler)**
el lápiz (pencil)	**el papel (paper)**
la cola (glue)	**las tijeras (scissors)**
la pluma (pen)	**el cuaderno (notebook)**

	ruler **la regla** lah rray–glah	**pencil** **el lápiz** el lah–pees
book **el libro** el lee–bro	**glue** **la cola** lah ko–lah	**scissors** **las tijeras** lahs tee–hay–rahs
paper **el papel** el pah–pel	**notebook** **el cuaderno** el kwah–der–no	**backpack** **la mochila** lah mo–chee–lah
pen **la pluma** lah plu–mah		

PARTS OF THE BODY

MATERIALS:

◆ paper

◆ crayons or colored pencils

◆ paste

◆ hole punch

◆ scissors

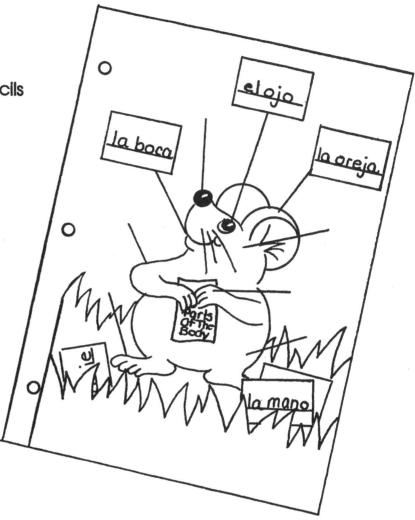

CONSTRUCTION:

1. Reproduce the patterns on pages 36 and 37 and hand them out for students to color and cut out.

2. Students paste the grass pattern (page 37) to the activity page (page 36). This will form a pocket for the word cards.

3. Punch three holes along the side of the activity page.

4. Have students insert the activity page in their booklets, write the name of the body part in English on the back of each card, and place the cards in the pocket.

5. Instruct the students to place the cards beside the appropriate lines on the activity page and then turn the cards over to self-check their answers.

6. Pronunciation cards for this activity are on page 38.

Cut out the grass pattern and then turn it over and color.

GLUE

Write the name of the body part on the back of each card.

el ojo
eye

la nariz
nose

la boca
mouth

la oreja
ear

la cabeza
head

el brazo
arm

la mano
hand

la pierna
leg

el pie
foot

eye **el ojo** el o–ho	**nose** **la nariz** lah nah–rees	**mouth** **la boca** lah bo–kah
ear **la oreja** lah o–ray–hah	**head** **la cabeza** lah kah–bay–sah	**arm** **el brazo** el brah–so
hand **la mano** lah mah–no	**leg** **la pierna** lah pyer–nah	**foot** **el pie** el pe–ay

FRUIT BASKET

MATERIALS:

- ◆ paper
- ◆ crayons or colored pencils
- ◆ paste
- ◆ hole punch
- ◆ scissors

la canasta

la fruta

la manzana

Back View

CONSTRUCTION:

1. Reproduce the activity patterns on pages 40–43 and hand them out.

2. Instruct students to color and cut out the activity page (page 40) and the basket pattern (page 41).

3. Students fold up the basket pattern along the dotted lines and paste the edges together. Then the basket is pasted to the activity page.

4. Punch three holes along the side of the activity page.

5. Have students insert the activity page in their booklets and then color and cut out the fruit patterns (pages 42 and 43).

6. Students should write the Spanish name for the fruit on the back of each pattern and place the fruit in the basket. Answers can be checked by turning over the fruit.

7. Pronunciation cards for this activity are on page 44.

GLUE BASKET HERE

la canasta

la fruta

GLUE

GLUE

41

la manzana
apple

las uvas
grapes

las fresas
strawberries

la naranja
orange

el melón
melon

el plátano
banana

el durazno
peach

43

grapes las uvas lahs oo–bahs	apple la manzana lah mahn–sah–nah	orange la naranja lah nah–ran–hah
strawberries las fresas lahs fray–sahs	melon el melón el may–lon	banana el plátano el plah–tah–no
peach el durazno el doo–rahs–no	basket la canasta lah kah–nahs–tah	fruit la fruta lah froo–tah

WORDS AND PHRASES

MATERIALS:

- ◆ paper
- ◆ crayons or colored pencils
- ◆ paste
- ◆ hole punch
- ◆ scissors

CONSTRUCTION:

1. Reproduce the activity patterns on pages 46 and 47 and hand them out for students to color and cut out.

2. Students paste the grass pattern (page 47) to the activity page (page 46). This will form a pocket for the cards.

3. Punch three holes along the side of the activity page.

4. Instruct the students to insert the activity page in their booklets.

5. Have students cut out the cards (pages 47–49) and place the cards in the pocket.

6. Instruct the students to review each card. The cards can be pulled out of the pockets to self-check the answers.

7. Pronunciation cards for this activity are on pages 50 and 51.

el sol

la hierba

Words
And
Phrases

GLUE

GLUE

GLUE

46   ©1995 by Incentive Publications, Inc., Nashville, TN.

sí yes	no no
¡hola! hello	¡adiós! good-bye

(muchas) gracias (many) thanks	de nada you are welcome
el maestro teacher (male)	la maestra teacher (female)
la escuela school	la aula classroom
el niño boy	la niña girl

el hermano brother	**la hermana** sister
el padre father	**la madre** mother
el abuelo grandfather	**la abuela** grandmother
la casa house	**feliz cumpleaños** happy birthday

hello!
¡hola!
oh-lah

you are welcome
de nada
deh nah-dah

school
la escuela
lah es-kway-lah

yes
sí
see

no
no
noh

(many) thanks
(muchas) gracias
moo-chahs grah-sy-ahs

teacher (female)
la maestra
lah mah-es-tra

boy
el niño
el nee-nyo

good-bye!
¡adiós!
ah-dy-os

teacher (male)
el maestro
el mah-es-tro

classroom
la aula
lah ow-lah

girl	brother	sister
la niña	**el hermano**	**la hermana**
lah nee-nyah	el er-mah-no	lah er-mah-nah

father	mother	grandfather
el padre	**la madre**	**el abuelo**
el pah-dray	lah mah-dray	el ah-bway-lo

grandmother	house	happy birthday
la abuela	**la casa**	**feliz cumpleaños**
lah ah-bway-lah	lah kah-sah	fay-lees koom-play-ah-nyos

sun	grass
el sol	**la hierba**
el sol	lah yer-bah

RESEARCH ACTIVITIES

MATERIALS:

- ◆ paper
- ◆ pencil
- ◆ crayons or colored pencils
- ◆ hole punch
- ◆ scissors

CONSTRUCTION:

(REPORT)

1. Reproduce and cut out the activity sheet on page 53. Hand out.
2. Assign or have each student choose a Spanish-speaking country to research. They will write the name of the country on the line provided and then write the report on the activity sheet.
3. Punch three holes along the side of the activity sheet. Students insert the activity sheet in their booklets.

(MAP AND FLAG)

1. Reproduce and cut out the activity sheet on page 54. Hand out.
2. Instruct each student to draw a map and a flag of the country he or she is researching.
3. Punch three holes along the side of the activity sheet. Students insert the activity sheet in their booklets.

(PHOTOGRAPHS)

1. Reproduce and cut out the activity sheet on page 55. Hand out.
2. Have the students draw pictures of famous landmarks on the "photographs" relating to their research papers. Instruct the students to write a brief description under each picture.
3. Punch three holes along the side of the activity sheet. Students insert the activity sheet in their booklets.

(POSTCARD)

1. Reproduce and cut out the activity sheet on page 56. Hand out.
2. Have each student draw a picture on the front of the "postcard" relating to his or her selected country. Instruct each student to write a letter to a friend on the back of the postcard.
3. Punch three holes along the side of the activity sheet. Students insert the activity sheet in their booklets.

These activities can be displayed on a bulletin board first and then inserted in the students' booklets.

Report

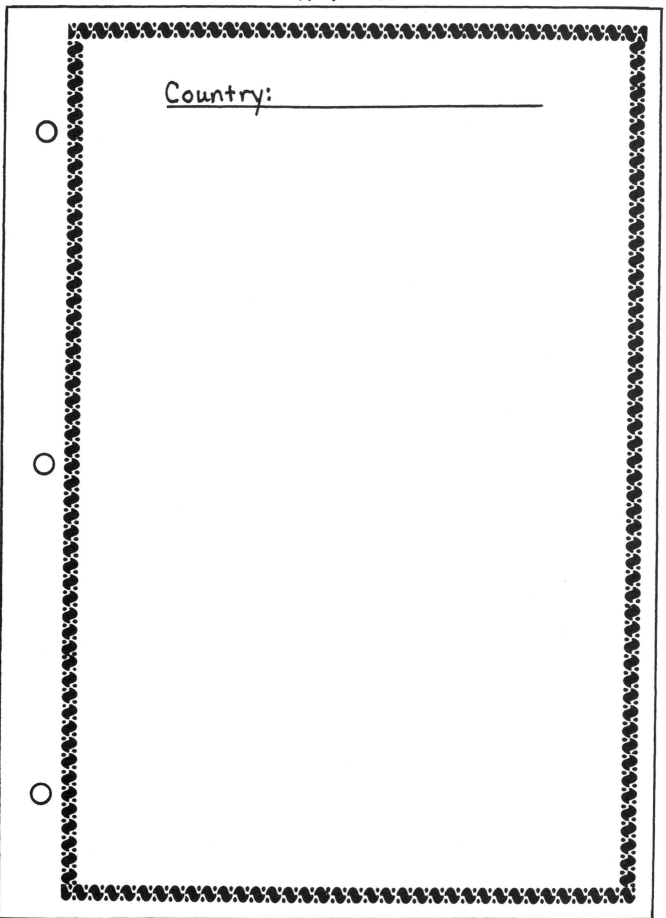

Country: _____

map
el mapa
(el mah-pah)

O

O

flag
la bandera
(lah bahn-day-rah)

O

photograph
la fotografía
(lah fo-to-grah-fee-ah)

postcard
la tarjeta postal
(lah tar-hay-tah pos-tahl)

CERTIFICATE

MATERIALS:

- ◆ paper
- ◆ crayons or colored pencils
- ◆ hole punch
- ◆ scissors

CONSTRUCTION:

1. Reproduce the certificates and personalize them by filling in the appropriate information (pattern, page 58).

2. Have each student color and cut out his or her certificate.

3. Punch three holes along the side of the certificate.

4. Students insert the certificate in their booklets.

Fantástico

Terrífico

Excelente

To: _____

From: _____

Date: _____

SPANISH CLASS IS TERRÍFICO

MATERIALS:

◆ construction paper

◆ crayons

◆ markers

◆ paste

◆ scissors

CONSTRUCTION:

1. Cover the bulletin board with blue paper.

2. Reproduce and color the patterns on pages 60–63.

3. Paste the ear pattern to the head pattern. Paste the head, feet, and tail patterns to the body.

4. Attach the mouse pattern to the bulletin board.

5. With a marker write "Spanish Class Is Terrífico" on the cheese pattern. Attach the cheese pattern to the bulletin board.

6. Display the students' work on the board.

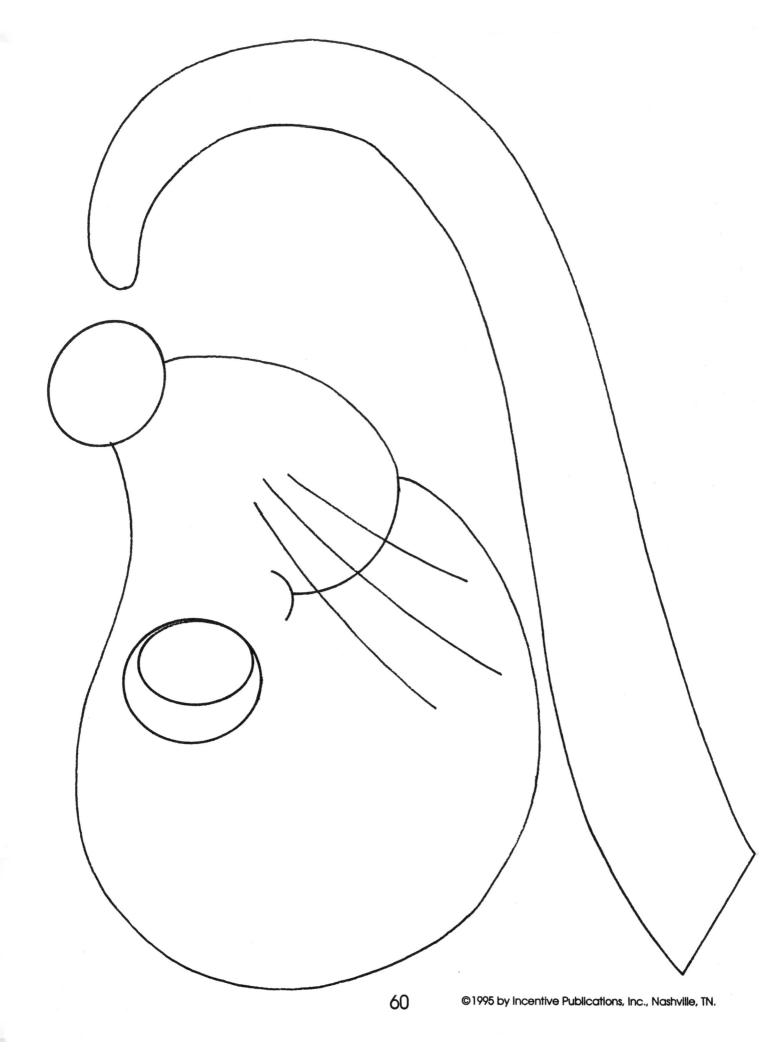

60

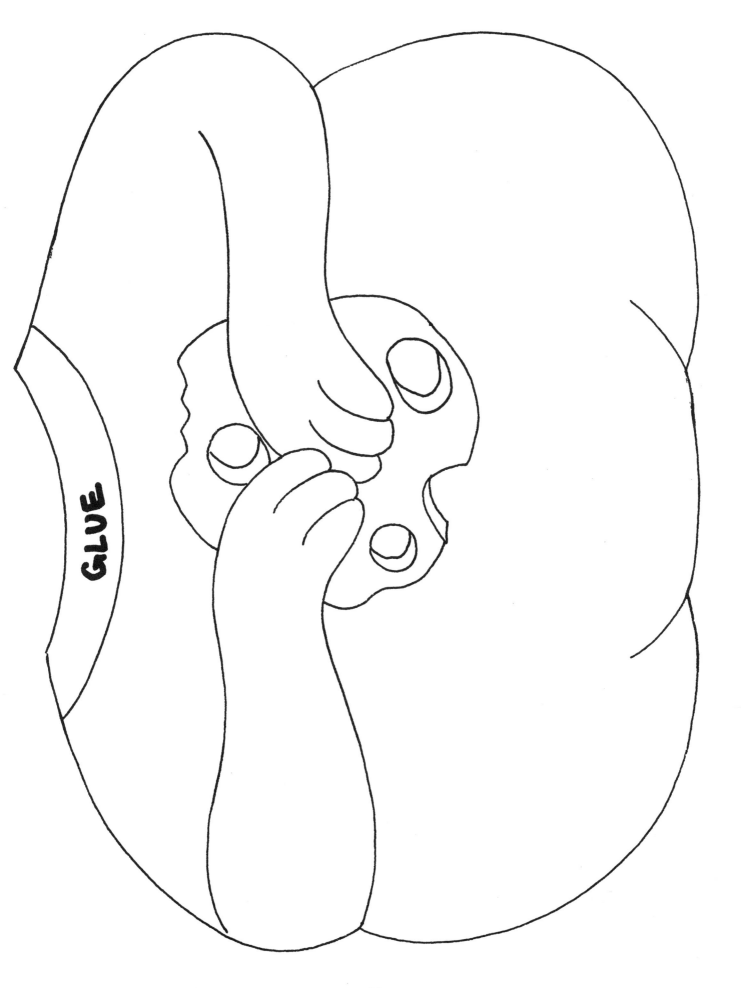

GLUE

61

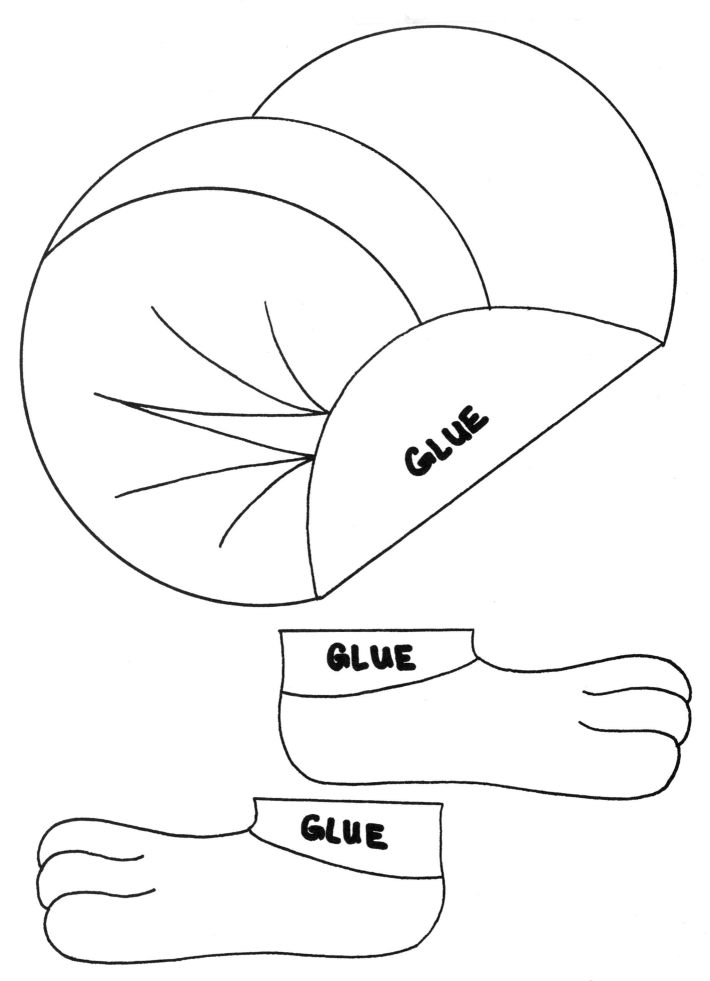

GLUE

GLUE

GLUE

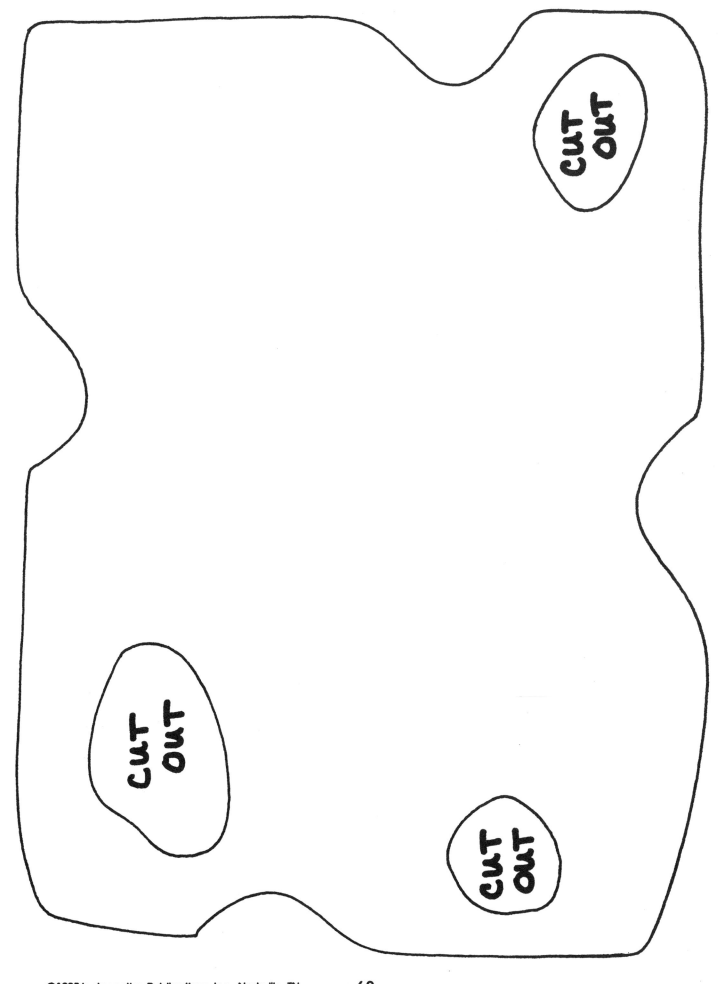